This book is dedicated to:

_____

© 2003 Havoc Publishing
San Diego, California
U.S.A.

Text by Maureen Webster

ISBN 0-7416-1260-7

www.havocpub.com

Made in China

Explore Your Wild Side

Take a hot bath . . .

It can take hours off a bad mood.

Take care of you . . .

It's the only way you can take care of others.

Define your success . . .

Don't accept others' definitions of life.

Speak it out loud . . .

"I can do whatever I want to!"

Imagine yourself
twenty years from now . . .

What will you wish you had spent more time doing?

What do YOU want?

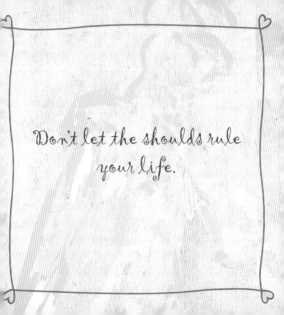

Don't let the shoulds rule
your life.

Practice saying "no" in front of a mirror.

No! No! No!

How would you
spend your day . . .

If you had the luxury to choose anything?

What would you like to
change?

In what areas of your life is change necessary?

Launch yourself into the
things that are missing in
your world . . .

Quirky just feels right.

This is the day . . .

To embark on an extravagant
life.

Your whole life is in front
of you . . .

What do you desire?

Carve out time . . .

For yourself.

Understand the difference
between smart and beautiful.

How can you create more
beauty in your life?

When was the last time that life made you feel like doing cartwheels?

How can you create more of that?

Don't wait around for the right things and people and opportunities to come to you . . .

Have fun with the wrong ones in the meantime!

Take a weekend getaway . . .

Give yourself the much-
needed gift of silence.

Open up to your dreams . . .

And they will become your
reality.

What are your questions?

Have you heard any answers?

What distinguishes your wants and needs?

"You only live once—but if you work it right, once is enough."

Joe E. Lewis

There's a BIG difference . . .

Between what a woman
wants and what she needs.

Who is the woman you were meant to be?

Step out of the box you have made for yourself.

Blessings arrive in unique
packages . . .

Friends, laughter, and chocolate.

Simple pleasures . . .

Can't happen often enough.

There's only one you . . .

Take care of yourself.

Use your emotions to point
your life in new directions.

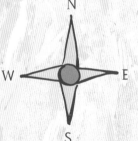

Why am I feeling like this?
What do I truly want?

Let yourself grow into the person you've always imagined.

"More important than how we live is how we spend each day."

Unknown

A day like today will never come again.

How will you mark it?

What memory can you offer?

Pay close attention to what
you love . . .

It's the little things that matter.

It's never too late to make a change in your life.

You are your own special gift.

Toss out the stress . . .

Find your untamed inner
self and unleash her.

Explore your wild side.

Wild women don't get the blues!

When is your next . . .

Go ahead . . . .

Dare yourself to be bold.

Keep the YES in your
attitude.

Be nothing short of
miraculous.

Passionate dreams . . .

Are what authentic life is
made of.

Be honest with yourself . . .

You know when it's time to bloom.

Change the way you feel . . .

By changing the way you act.

Feel your amazing power.